EUROPE

ASIA

Pastedown

North
Pacific Ocean

Indian
Ocean

AUSTRALIA

Southern
Ocean

ANTARCTICA

To Emmanuelle, who helped and inspired.—W.S.
For all kids, everywhere.—C.E.

STERLING CHILDREN'S BOOKS
New York

An Imprint of Sterling Publishing Co., Inc.
1166 Avenue of the Americas
New York, NY 10036

ISBN 978-1-4549-3213-0

Distributed in Canada by Sterling Publishing Co., Inc.
c/o Canadian Manda Group, 664 Annette Street
Toronto, Ontario M6S 2C8, Canada
Distributed in the United Kingdom by GMC Distribution Services
Castle Place, 166 High Street, Lewes, East Sussex BN7 1XU, England
Distributed in Australia by NewSouth Books
University of New South Wales, Sydney, NSW 2052, Australia

For information about custom editions, special sales, and premium and corporate purchases,
please contact Sterling Special Sales at 800-805-5489 or specialsales@sterlingpublishing.com.

Manufactured in China

Lot #:
2 4 6 8 10 9 7 5 3 1
12/18

sterlingpublishing.com

Cover and interior design by Heather Kelly

Photo credits—see page 33

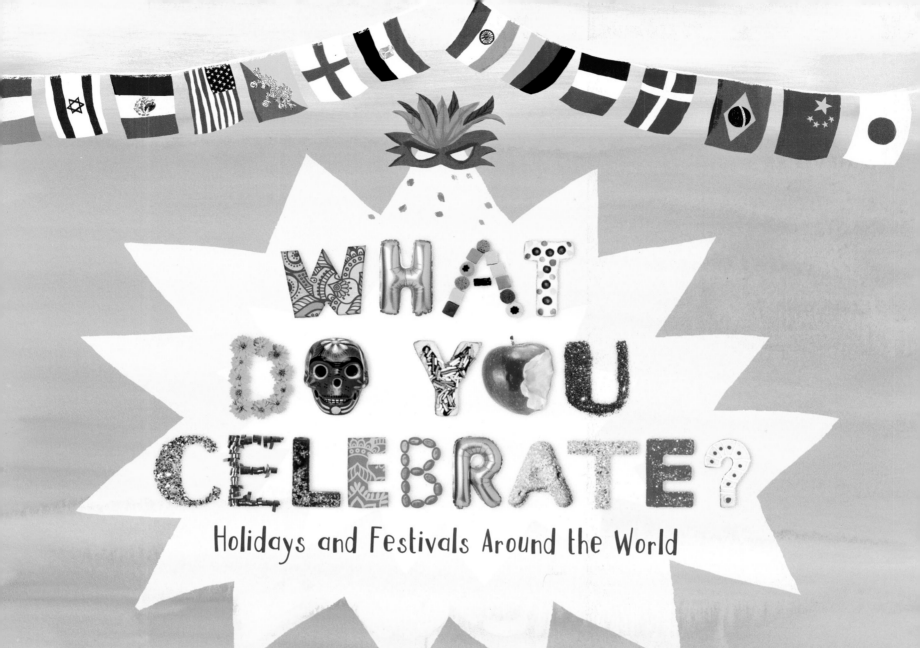

WHAT DO YOU CELEBRATE?

Holidays and Festivals Around the World

by **Whitney Stewart**

illustrated by **Christiane Engel**

STERLING CHILDREN'S BOOKS
New York

HOLIDAYS AND FESTIVALS AROUND THE WORLD

Holidays are so much fun! Do you know why people celebrate them? We have so many different reasons. Some holidays are for honoring historic events and important anniversaries. Others are for celebrating religion. Most holidays are wrapped up in tradition and are tied to the past. People add special foods and celebrations to make holidays memorable and exciting. This is true across the globe! Every country has days that are special, and you can explore many of them in this book. Get ready to travel the world and join the celebration!

Did you know that many holidays are according to a lunar calendar? Since the lunar year is approximately 354 days, that means some holidays don't fall on the same date every year, or sometimes even the same month.

CARNAVAL (CARNIVAL)
Late February or early March

HOLI
March

XIN NIAN (CHINESE NEW YEAR)
January or February

PURIM
Late winter

JANUARY · FEBRUARY · MARCH · APRIL · MAY · JUNE

FASTELAVN
February, the day before the start of Lent

EID AL-FITR
At the end of the month of Ramadan

HANAMI (CHERRY BLOSSOM FESTIVAL)
Late March or early April

FOOD DONATIONS

DANGPAI LOSAR
February or March

⚠️ A NOTE BEFORE YOU COOK & CRAFT ⚠️

Cooking and creating crafts are fun, but accidents can happen if you're not careful. Protecting yourself when you use the oven, hot pans, scissors, staplers, and sticks is important. Ask an adult first before using kitchen or craft tools.

GUY FAWKES DAY
Nov 5

FOURTH OF JULY
July 4

HALLOWEEN
Oct 31

JULY · AUGUST · SEPTEMBER · OCTOBER · NOVEMBER · DECEMBER

LATERNENFEST (LANTERN FESTIVAL)
Nov 11

LA FÊTE NATIONALE (BASTILLE DAY)
July 14

DIA DE LOS MUERTOS (DAY OF THE DEAD)
Nov 1-2

XIN NIAN (CHINESE NEW YEAR)—CHINA

The legend behind Xin Nian (shin nyan), or Chinese New Year, has to do with a hungry beast named Nian. On the first night of the new year, Nian used to come down from the mountains and eat anything he could find in the villages—grains, animals, and even people. The frightened villagers hid in their homes until Nian went away. One day, an old man told the villagers that Nian was afraid of three things: loud noises, fire, and the color red. So, the next time Nian came, the villagers were ready. They had decorated their houses in red and put on red clothing. When the beast approached, they lit firecrackers and pounded on drums to scare Nian away for good.

Xin Nian is China's biggest and most important celebration of the year. It takes place in January or February, and the celebrations last for a week or longer. To start the year off with good fortune, families decorate their homes with red paper cuttings, lanterns, and banners with the Chinese character for good luck on them. Throughout New Year's Day, people wear red clothes and feast on such foods as whole fish, dumplings, noodles, and nian gao, a Xin Nian dessert. Adults give children hong bao—red envelopes filled with money. Many neighborhoods have parades, during which everyone pounds their drums and lights firecrackers to keep Nian away. The holiday ends under a full moon with a festival that often includes a dancing dragon, acrobats, and martial arts performers.

HOLIDAY TRADITIONS:

"GUO NIAN HAO" (gwo nyan how): Have a happy New Year!

NIAN GAO (nyan kow): traditional Xin Nian cake made from rice flour

NIAN HUA (nyan hwa): colored woodblock prints used for decoration during Xin Nian

HONG BAO (HONE bow): red envelopes of money given on special occasions

CHINESE DRUM
YOU WILL NEED (PER DRUM):

- 2 small paper plates
- 1 dowel or chopstick
- Red and gold paint
- Masking tape
- Red string or ribbon
- 2 small bells (beads can substitute)
- Stapler

INSTRUCTIONS:
Paint the backs of two paper plates in red and gold. When the paint is dry, turn over one plate and tape down the dowel or chopstick along the middle line, leaving a part below for you to hold. Cut the red string into two equal pieces, each about half the width of the plate. Tie each piece to a small bell. Tape the ends of the strings without bells to the midpoint of the plate, one on each side of the dowel. Leaving the bells hanging out, cover this plate with the other (painted sides out) and staple the edges together. Make sure you staple over the spot where the strings are attached to keep them in place. Now add decorations if you wish, and your drum is ready. By rubbing the dowel back in forth in your hands, you can make the bells swing and hit the drum. Or, hold the dowel and twist your hand so the bells beat the drum.

Nian Gao

Hong Bao

Nian Hua

DANGPAI LOSAR—BHUTAN

In Bhutan, a small Himalayan country, Losar (LO-sar) celebrations take place at different times in different parts of the country. Losar means "new year," and is often celebrated when the seasons are changing.

The largest New Year celebration is Dangpai Losar (DANG-bee LO-sar), which takes place on the first day of the first Bhutanese month, usually in February or March. Dangpai Losar is a national holiday, a time for singing, dancing, playing games, and spending time with friends and family. At dawn, families prepare breakfast foods like thuep (red rice porridge), desi (sweetened rice with saffron, cashews, and raisins), or shamday (salty rice with meat and eggs). They also drink suja (salty butter tea) or ngaja (sweet milk tea), served with zow (roasted rice) or gyaza sip (roasted maize). After feasting, people take the fun outdoors for matches of dha (archery), khuru (darts), or degor, a target game with stones. Children often receive new clothes at Losar; a kira for girls, and a gho for boys. People believe their behavior during this holiday sets the tone for the whole year. So by being friendly and generous during Losar, you are more likely to enjoy a peaceful year!

HOLIDAY TRADITIONS:

DHA (dha): archery, Bhutan's national sport

ZOW (zow): roasted rice dish

KIRA (KEE-ra): traditional dress for Bhutanese women

GHO (gho): traditional knee-length robe for Bhutanese men

DEGOR (SIMPLIFIED VERSION)
YOU WILL NEED:

- One target peg (or stick)
- A small beanbag toy per player
- A ruler

INSTRUCTIONS:

Degor can be played by individuals or teams. In Bhutan, players throw stones as close as possible to a target peg in the ground. This simplified version replaces stones with beanbags. Find a space outside where you can put a peg or stick in the ground as a target. Each player has a beanbag. If you have four or more players, form two teams. Players stand in a tossing zone ten feet away from the target. The first player tosses a beanbag underhand as close to the target as possible. Then the opponent takes a turn. For teams, go back and forth until all players have tossed their beanbags. After all players have finished tossing, score the round. Keep scoring rounds until a player (or team) reaches fifteen points, and wins. SCORING: A beanbag must land within eight inches of the target to score a point (use the ruler). If more than one beanbag lands within eight inches, only the closest one scores the point. If multiple beanbags land at *exactly* the same distance from the target, they cancel each other out and earn no points. A team can score multiple points in a round only if it has more than one beanbag within eight inches of the target while the other team has none.

Zow

Dha

Kira & Gho

Bhutan

CARNAVAL (CARNIVAL)—BRAZIL

Carnaval (can-na-VOW) occurs in late February or early March and is Brazil's biggest celebration of the year. The origin of the word carnaval means "putting away meat," which makes sense because it occurs right before the start of Lent, a forty-day period leading up to Easter during which many Christians give up eating meat and certain other foods. Carnaval traditions that people love are singing, dancing, throwing parties, and eating rich foods before they give them up for Lent.

Brazilians celebrate Carnaval in different ways. In Rio de Janeiro, they dance in a samba parade. Samba dancers make fast, rhythmic steps to a lively beat and add swaying motions with their arms. The dancers, musicians, and flag bearers of different samba schools all wear colorful costumes and compete for prizes. In other parts of the country, people throw outdoor parties with music, dancing, and feasts. Some families may decide to take their parties to the beach. In the state of Bahia, giant floats called trios elétricos roll along streets carrying musical performers. People follow behind, stopping for street food as they celebrate late into the night.

HOLIDAY TRADITIONS:

SAMBA (SAM-ba): Brazilian dance of African origin

TRIO ELÉTRICO (triu e-LECT-ri-ku): truck or float with performers on stage

ESPETINHOS (es-PET-cheen-os): Brazilian barbecued foods served on a stick or skewer

QUEIJO COALHO (KAY-joo cu-AL-loo): curd cheese, often grilled and served on a stick or skewer

CARNAVAL MASK

YOU WILL NEED:

- 1 paper plate, any color
- Scissors
- Markers in assorted colors
- Decorations (glitter, stickers, feathers, ribbons, and more)
- Glue
- Stapler
- Thin wooden dowel
- Duct tape

INSTRUCTIONS:

Cut the paper plate in half. Have a friend make a mask with the other half. Turn the half so the straight edge is at the bottom and draw two holes for your eyes and a semicircle at the center of the bottom edge for your nose. Using the scissors, cut the eye holes and the semicircular nose hole. Decorate the outside of your plate (the side that bulges outward) with markers and whatever other materials you have on hand, using glue if needed. Tape the dowel to the inside edge of the plate to use as a handle.

Get your friends together and have your own Carnaval parade!

Espetinhos

Samba

Queijo Coalho

Brazil

FASTELAVN—DENMARK

Fastelavn (fest-e-LOWN) comes from an old word that means the "evening before the fast." This Danish holiday was originally connected to the Christian celebration of Lent. The night before the fast, Danish people would be festive and eat heartily, and even though this holiday has become less religious over the years, Fastelavn is still celebrated this way. In February, bakers fill their shop windows with Fastelavnsboller, cream-filled puff pastries, which people buy for Fastelavn parties.

On Fastelavn morning, Danish children often wake up grown-ups by tapping their bed with a decorated bundle of twigs called a Fastelavnsris. Then they dress up in costume and get ready for a day filled with parties. One party tradition is to hang up a barrel with a black cat painted on it. A black cat represents the winter darkness that must go away before spring can come. The barrel is full of sweets, and children take turns hitting it with a stick until it breaks open and candy pours out. The lucky person who opens the barrel is named the queen of cats, and the person who knocks the barrel to the ground is named the king! In some towns, kids take the celebration to the streets by going door to door, singing Fastelavn songs and asking for money or treats.

HOLIDAY TRADITIONS:

FASTELAVNSBOLLER (fest-e-LOWNS-boll-er): Fastelavn sweet buns

FASTELAVN UDKLÆDNING (fest-e-LOWN OOTH-kleth-ning): Fastelavn costume

FASTELAVNSTØNDE (fest-e-LOWNS-tuh-na): decorated barrel full of sweets

FASTELAVNSRIS (fest-e-LOWNS-rees): traditional bundle of twigs that kids use to tease grown-ups

MAKE A FASTELAVNSTØNDE

YOU WILL NEED:

- A large empty cardboard box with a lid or foldable sides
- Black markers or crayons
- Candy
- Hole-punch or scissors
- String
- Tape
- Stick or pole

INSTRUCTIONS:

Draw black cats all over the box and fill it with bite-size candy or treats. Punch or cut two holes at the top of the box and thread string through it. Tape the box shut. Suspend the box from a tree branch or pole. Take turns swinging the stick at the box to try to smash it open. When the queen of cats breaks open the box, pick up as much candy as you can. Keep taking turns hitting the box until the king of cats knocks it down completely.

Fastelavstønde

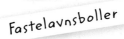

Fastelavnsboller

Fastelavnsris

DENMARK

FASTELAVN SONG

Fastelavn is my name,
Buns I want.
If I get no buns,
I will make trouble.
Buns up, buns down
Buns in my tummy.
If I get no buns,
I will make trouble.

PURIM—ISRAEL

In Israel, Jewish people celebrate Purim (POOR-im) in late winter. On Purim, Jewish families go to synagogue, a Jewish house of worship, to hear the biblical Book of Esther, which tells how the Jews of Persia were saved from Haman. This evil prime minister secretly planned to kill all the Jews, and the king would have gone along with it if not for his wife, Queen Esther, who courageously revealed Haman's evil and that she herself was Jewish. The king punished Haman with death and appointed Esther's uncle, Mordechai, to take Haman's place. During the reading, listeners boo, hiss, and shake groggers (noisemakers) to drown out Haman's name.

A theme of Purim is that situations can turn around dramatically. Haman wanted the Jewish people of Persia to be killed, but instead they were saved and he died. In Israel, even Jewish people who are not religious join Purim festivities by dressing as clowns, superheroes, and more and attending daytime parades. Amid the fun, Purim also has a message of generosity. People exchange food with one another and make donations to those in need.

HOLIDAY TRADITIONS:

HAMANTASCHEN (HA-mahn-ta-shen): "Haman's pockets," triangular shaped pastries with filling, eaten during Purim

MEGILLAH (meh-GILL-ah): Hebrew for "scroll," refers to the Book of Esther, read aloud on Purim

MISHLOACH MANOT (MEE-shloh-ach mah-NOHT): Purim gift baskets, Hebrew for "sending of portions"

GROGGER (GROG-ger): rattle that people shake to drown out Haman's name during the reading of the megillah

HAMANTASCHEN
(Makes about 25—30 cookies, depending upon their size)

YOU WILL NEED:

- 3 eggs
- 3/4 cup sugar
- 1/2 cup cooking oil
- 1 tablespoon orange or lemon zest
- 1 teaspoon vanilla
- Juice of half a lemon
- 1/4 cup warm water
- 4 cups flour
- 1/2 teaspoon salt
- 3 teaspoons baking powder
- 1 cup of thick jam (any flavor) for the filling

INSTRUCTIONS:

Preheat oven to 375° F. Beat eggs and sugar. Add the rest of the wet ingredients, except the jam, and mix well. Stir in the flour, salt, and baking powder until dough is smooth but not sticky. Refrigerate the dough for an hour. Divide the dough into two parts. Lightly flour a smooth, clean surface. Roll out one part of your dough at a time to about 1/8-inch thick, keeping the other half refrigerated. Cut out circles with a round cookie cutter or cup. Fill each circle with 1/2—1 teaspoon jam in the middle. (Don't use too much or it will spill out while baking.)

Fold the circle along three edges to make a triangle-shaped cookie with jam peeking through the center. Pinch the three corners of the cookie to hold the filling and keep the cookie's shape during baking. Place your hamantaschen on a greased or coated baking sheet and bake for 20—25 minutes, or until golden brown. Let cool.

These cookies are traditionally made with poppy seed or prune filling but are also popular with other flavors of jam or even chocolate chips.

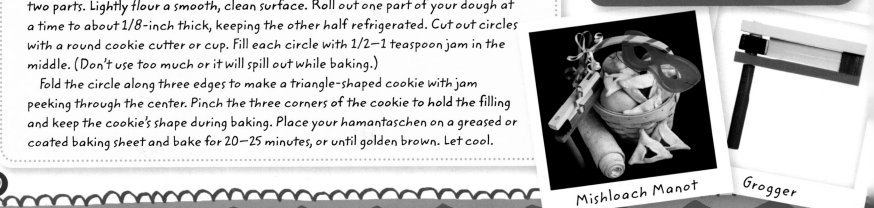

Mishloach Manot

Grogger

HANAMI (CHERRY BLOSSOM FESTIVAL)—JAPAN

According to Japanese legend, a fairy named Konohana-Sakuyahime hovers in the sky and awakens cherry blossoms every spring with her delicate breath. The flowering trees inspired Japanese emperors to establish a tradition of blossom-viewing parties called Hanami, at which people would recite poems about the lovely blooms. Hanami became more popular in the 1700s after the Shogun (military ruler) Tokugawa Yoshimune had cherry trees planted along the rivers and hillsides of Tokyo. The pink, white, yellow, or green blossoms last only about two weeks, but they always return the following year. They are a symbol of the cycle of life, death, and rebirth, and they remind people that things will always come and go.

Each year in Japan, newspapers announce where and when to see the cherry blossoms and attend Hanami festivals. In big cities like Tokyo and Osaka, the festivals usually take place at the end of March or early in April. People pack picnics and eat under the trees. Or, they paddle boats along tree-lined rivers and canals and glide over the blossoms' reflections on the water. For nighttime viewing, called yozakura, people hang paper lanterns in the trees to light up the blossoms in the dark.

HOLIDAY TRADITIONS:

HANAMI (ha-NA-mi): flower-viewing parties

SAKURA ANPAN (SA-ku-ra AN-pahn): Japanese sweet made with shiro-an (sweetened white bean paste) mixed with chopped salted cherry blossom leaves

SAKURAMOCHI (SA-ku-ra MO-chee): sweet pink-colored rice cake with a red bean paste center, and wrapped in a pickled cherry blossom leaf

SAKURA (SA-ku-ra): cherry blossom

HANAMI

YOU WILL NEED:
- Poems about spring
- Friends

INSTRUCTIONS:
Organize your own Hanami by hosting an outdoor poetry reading. Before your Hanami, let the beauty of spring inspire you, and write your own poems about it. What does springtime mean to you? How does it make you feel? Print out your poems and ask your friends to do the same. Under the shade of a flowering tree (in your backyard or at a park), sit in a circle and take turns reading your poems out loud.

Bonus: Read translations of poems by famous Japanese poets Kobayashi Issa, Matsuo Bashō, Masaoka Shiki, and Yosa Buson.

Or, print out these well-known poems about spring:

- "Dear March, Come In" by Emily Dickinson
- "Spring is like a perhaps hand" by e. e. cummings
- "Daffodowndilly" by A. A. Milne
- "A Rain Song" by Evaleen Stein
- "Caterpillar" by Christina Rossetti

Spring is here

Sakura Anpan

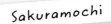
Sakuramochi

Sakura

Japan

HOLI—INDIA

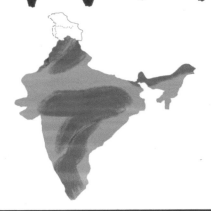

Also called the Festival of Colors, Holi (HO-lee) takes place in March and marks the beginning of spring. It is tied to different Indian legends, one of which involves King Hiranyakashyap (heer-ah-nee-KA-shyap), an evil king who ordered people to worship him instead of the Hindu gods. The king's son Prahlad was so devoted to the Hindu god Vishnu that he refused to follow his father's order. Because of this, the angry king demanded his son be killed, but every time someone tried to kill Prahlad, Vishnu saved him. Finally, the king's sister Holika pulled Prahlad into a fire and held him there. She thought her own magic would keep her safe from the fire, but Vishnu rescued Prahlad once again, and Holika burned to ashes. This legend represents the victory of good over evil. To remember this on the eve before Holi, families make bonfires and roast popcorn, chickpeas, grains, or coconuts as offerings to the gods. Sometimes they even burn a picture of the evil Holika.

Another legend connected to Holi is that of the fun-loving god Krishna, who drenched his companion Radha and her friends with brightly colored water. This is why, on the day of Holi, people follow in the tradition of Krishna and Radha by spraying each other with gulal (color powder) and having playful water fights. The streets fill up with people singing and dancing, and nobody escapes without a splash of color.

HOLIDAY TRADITIONS:

GULAL (goo-LAL): colored powders used at Holi

HOLIKA PYRE (HO-lee-ka pire): pile of branches and cow dung, often with a picture of Holika on top, to be burned for Holi celebrations

PICHKARI (pich-KA-ree): squirt gun used at Holi to spray colors

RANGOLI (ran-GO-lee): colorful patterns that reflect happiness, often seen outside homes and in public places during Holi

COLORFUL WATER FIGHT
YOU WILL NEED

- White oversize T-shirt
- Goggles, nose clip, and swim cap (optional)
- One squirt gun per person
- Water
- Small bowls
- Plant-based liquid coloring
- Plant-based color powders

INSTRUCTIONS:
Dress in a white oversize T-shirt. If you're worried about getting color in your eyes, nose, or hair, wear goggles, a nose clip, and a swim cap. Fill squirt guns with water colored with natural dyes. Fill several small bowls with color powder. Grab a handful of powder and, when everyone is ready, throw the powder at each other and spray each other with the water. Keep playing until everyone is covered in color. Display the shirt in your room as a keepsake!

Gulal

Holika Pyre

Rangoli

India

EID AL-FITR—EGYPT

Fourteen hundred years ago in Mecca (in what is now Saudi Arabia), the prophet Muhammad was alone in the wilderness when the angel Gabriel came to him with messages from God. Muhammad then taught others what he had learned. His teachings were collected in a book called the Qur'an, which is sacred in the religion of Islam. One of Muhammad's most important teachings is that people should fast during the daylight hours of the holy month of Ramadan. This means that many Muslim people in Egypt who are healthy enough to fast do not eat or drink between sunrise and sunset.

At the end of the month of Ramadan, upon the first sighting of the new moon, Muslim people in Egypt celebrate Eid al-Fitr (EED-ul-fitr), which means the "festival of breaking the fast." On this first day of Eid, people gather outside or at a mosque (a Muslim place of worship) for early morning prayers, and later, they share a special meal with their families. The streets become crowded with people celebrating. For the next two days, people enjoy visiting relatives and friends, strolling through parks, or just relaxing. Children wear new clothes and receive Eidyah (eed-ya), which are gifts of money. When people greet each other, they like to say, "Eid Mubarak!" which means, "Have a blessed Eid!"

HOLIDAY TRADITIONS:

"EID MUBARAK!" (EED moo-BAR-ek): "Have a blessed Eid!"

KAHK (kahk): nut cookie with powdered sugar eaten during Eid al-Fitr

ZAKAT AL-FITR (za-KAT ul-fitr): mandatory act of charity for Eid al-Fitr

SALAT AL-EID (SAL-at ul eed): Eid prayer

A big part of Eid al-Fitr is inclusiveness, or making sure that everyone is able to join in the fun. During every cheerful holiday, there are people who are struggling and unable to participate. The next holiday you celebrate, consider giving to those in need. You can start your own holiday food drive in your community or school.

HOLIDAY FOOD DRIVE

YOU WILL NEED:

- Food collection boxes
- Poster boards
- 8-1/2 x 11 sheets of paper for fliers
- Markers
- Volunteers

INSTRUCTIONS:

Form a group of volunteers, and together, answer four important questions: (1) Where you will hold your food drive? (2) Where you will donate your food? (3) What kinds of food (fresh, cooked, or canned) can be donated? (4) How long will your food drive run? Next, decorate your food collection boxes, and make posters and fliers to promote your food drive. Announce your food drive and ask people to donate. You may be able to give a short speech about it at a school or club assembly. When the drive is over, ask an adult for help delivering the donated food to a food bank or food pantry that will distribute it.

FOOD DONATIONS

Kahk

"Eid Mubarak!"

FOURTH OF JULY—UNITED STATES

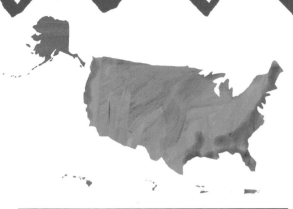

In the 1600s, people from Great Britain sailed across the Atlantic Ocean and settled among people living in tribes on land that is now the United States. Those English settlers then built thirteen colonies, and even though they were far away from Great Britain, they were still ruled by the British king. The colonists grew frustrated with the king who made them live under unfair laws that they could not change. One of these laws said the colonists had to pay high taxes on tea, molasses, and various goods that came from Britain and other countries. Eventually, the colonists became fed up and decided to form their own government. On July 4, 1776, leaders from the colonies approved a Declaration of Independence, a document stating that the colonies would no longer be part of Britain. The colonists then fought the British in the Revolutionary War—and won! They called their newly independent country the United States of America.

Every year, Americans celebrate the Fourth of July, also called Independence Day, with barbecues, banners, and parades. People often wear the colors of the American flag (red, white, and blue) and play patriotic songs like the "Star Spangled Banner." When the sun goes down and day becomes night, fireworks explode in the sky, reminding people all over the country of their freedom and of the people who fought for it over two centuries ago.

HOLIDAY TRADITIONS:

BARBECUE (BAR-be-kyu): way of cooking over an open source of heat, like hot coals

FIREWORKS (FI-er-works): objects that use explosive material to make a loud noise or display of light

LIBERTY BELL (LI-ber-tee bell): on every Fourth of July, descendants of the signers of the Declaration of Independence gently tap this giant bell in Philadelphia thirteen times to honor the patriots from the thirteen original colonies

RED, WHITE, AND BLUE PARFAIT
(Makes six servings)
YOU WILL NEED:

- 8 ounces vanilla or plain low-fat yogurt
- 1/2 teaspoon vanilla
- 4 ounces whipped cream, fresh or store-bought
- 3 cups fresh raspberries and/or cut-up fresh strawberries
- 3 cups fresh blueberries
- 6 American flag toothpicks, one per parfait

INSTRUCTIONS:
Rinse the fruit and pat dry with paper towels. In a large bowl, stir together the yogurt and vanilla. Fold in the whipped cream. To serve, in six 12-ounce glasses, alternate layers of the berries with layers of the yogurt mixture. Finish by poking an American flag toothpick into a berry on top.

Liberty Bell

Barbecue

Fireworks

UNITED STATES

LA FÊTE NATIONALE (BASTILLE DAY)—FRANCE

Some say that in the late 1700s, when Queen Marie Antoinette of France heard that French people didn't even have bread to eat, she responded, "Let them eat cake!" There's no proof the queen actually said this, but it's a popular story that shows how little she and King Louis XVI understood the needs of the people. Many were poor and starving, and eventually—outraged that the king and queen weren't doing anything to help—the people called for a new type of government. On July 14, 1789, thousands marched in the streets. An angry crowd stormed into the Bastille prison in Paris, freeing prisoners and taking gunpowder. This day marked the beginning of the French Revolution, which lasted for ten years. During this time, people fought for a new government that would give them more rights.

Today, la Fête Nationale or, Bastille Day, is celebrated all over France on July 14th. In the morning, a military parade goes down the famous Avenue des Champs-Élysées in Paris, the capital of France. At the end of the parade, the French president gives a speech about liberté (freedom), égalité (equality), and fraternité (brotherhood, or togetherness). People throughout the country enjoy picnics, street festivals, and fireworks to honor these important values.

HOLIDAY TRADITIONS:

AVENUE DES CHAMPS-ÉLYSÉES (AH-ven-new day CHANZ-eh-lee-zay)—famous avenue in France known for its museums, restaurants, and shops

LE CHÂTEAU DE VERSAILLES (le CHA-toh de VER-si-ee): palace where King Louis XVI and Queen Marie Antoinette lived before the French Revolution

LA MARSEILLAISE (la MAR-say-yez): French national anthem often played on la Fête Nationale

PLACE DE LA BASTILLE (plahs de la BA-stee): square in Paris where the Bastille prison stood before it was destroyed during the French Revolution

LA FÊTE NATIONALE PICNIC

YOU WILL NEED:

- Baguette (French bread)
- French cheeses (Camembert, Brie, Comte, etc.)
- Ham slices or sausage
- Fresh fruit (apples and pears go well with cheese)
- Dessert (like chocolate or raisins)
- Paper plates
- Napkins
- Blanket
- French stories

INSTRUCTIONS:

Pack all your food items into a picnic basket. Carry the baguette and blanket separately. Invite some friends and choose a picnic spot outdoors where you can spread out your blanket. Lay out all your food and dig in! After you eat, read aloud French stories like *Madeline, The Story of Babar, Beauty and the Beast,* or *The Tales of Mother Goose.* If you speak French, read them in the original language.

Le Château de Versailles

La Marseillaise

HALLOWEEN—IRELAND

Halloween finds its roots in an ancient harvest festival in Ireland called Samhain (SAH-ween), which marked the beginning of the new year. Villagers believed that on this October night, ghosts could pass through our world on their way to the next. People often disguised themselves in all white to look like ghosts, so that evil spirits would not bother them. They also built bonfires and left food outside to keep spirits happy on their journey. To light up the night, villagers carved lanterns out of gourds, and called them jack-o'-lanterns. This tradition began with the legend of an old blacksmith named Jack who died and wandered in darkness with nothing but a burning coal inside a carved-out turnip for a lantern. Christianity eventually began to promote All Hallows' Eve—"hallows" meaning "saints" in Old English—which falls around the same time as Samhain. The holiday became popular and is known now as Halloween, a favorite holiday in many countries.

Today in Ireland, people celebrate Halloween by parading in scary costumes, lighting bonfires, and carving jack-o'-lanterns with spooky faces. Children go door to door asking for candy (also known as trick or treating) and play games like Snap Apple. Just remember, the next time you're out on Halloween, keep your eyes open for Ol' Jack!

HOLIDAY TRADITIONS:

JACK-O'-LANTERN (JAK-oh-lan-tern): lantern usually carved from a pumpkin to look like a face

COLCANNON (KOHL-can-non): traditional Irish cabbage and potato dish eaten during Halloween

BARMBRACK (BARM-brak): sweet bread with dried fruit

SNAP APPLE
YOU WILL NEED:

- One apple per person
- String to hang up apples
- Tree branch or rope from which to hang apples

INSTRUCTIONS:
Attach strings to the stems of the apples and hang them from a tree branch or a rope tied between trees. Add as many apples as you have players. (You can also use donuts, which are easier to bite.) Players stand with hands behind their backs and try to bite the apple in front of them. The first person to take a bite wins. To raise the stakes, make the rule that the first person to eat a whole apple wins.

Jack-o'-lanterns

Colcannon

Barmbrack

DÍA DE LOS MUERTOS (DAY OF THE DEAD)—MEXICO

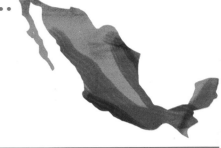

Día de los Muertos, or the Day of the Dead, is a holiday when the people of Mexico honor loved ones who have died. The tradition began thousands of years ago with ancient s—particularly the Aztec and Toltec peoples—who believed the souls of the dead returned to visit their living relatives.

Today in Mexico, the holiday takes place over two days. On November 1, people welcome the spirits of children, and the next day, they welcome the spirits of adults. People create offering tables for the spirits, called ofrendas, which are set up in homes, churches, cemeteries, and other public places. An ofrenda is usually draped with a papel picado (tissue paper cut into detailed designs) and covered with foods and beverages to satisfy the hungry and thirsty spirits. Families also decorate the ofrenda with marigolds, candles, incense, and photographs. Pan de muerto (bread of the dead) is a special holiday treat. Brightly colored calaveras (skulls) made of sugar or candy, and catrinas (skeletons) are popular symbols on this day. People like to keep the holiday cheerful by painting their faces like skulls or dressing as skeletons as they parade through the streets.

DÍA DE LOS MUERTOS MARSHMALLOW SKULLS

YOU WILL NEED:

- A bag of marshmallows
- Large chocolate sprinkles or licorice strips
- Edible decorating markers
- Cake icing (vanilla)
- Natural food coloring
- Ice cream sticks or lollipop sticks
- Small jar

INSTRUCTIONS:

Poke three chocolate sprinkles or licorice strips into a marshmallow for eyes and a nose. With edible markers, draw a skull mouth (one long horizontal line and three short vertical lines that intersect the horizontal line) and add flowers or patterns around the eyes and forehead. If you want, mix a small portion of vanilla frosting with food coloring and use it to decorate as well. Use these skull designs as inspiration. Place your marshmallow skulls on sticks and display them in a small jar.

Ofrenda with Calaveras

Catrín/Catrina

Papel Picado

GUY FAWKES DAY—ENGLAND

In November 1605, thirteen men plotted to blow up a government building in London, England, and kill King James I. The king's men learned of this "Gunpowder Plot" and arrested Guy Fawkes, who was caught in a storeroom carrying long fuses to set the barrels of gunpowder on fire. The king's men were lucky they were able to stop the plot and avoid a deadly explosion. The people in London lit bonfires to celebrate the failed plot, and since then, November 5th has been a day of thanksgiving. Over time, people started calling it Guy Fawkes Day or, more commonly, Bonfire Night.

In England, people celebrate this holiday with parades, fireworks, and bonfires. Families build giant piles of wood and place a life-size dummy of Guy Fawkes (called simply a "Guy") on top before setting the whole thing on fire. Around the bonfire, people eat soup, sausages, and hamburgers. They sweeten the night with toffee apples or sticky ginger cake called parkin. You might also see people in the streets dressed up to look like Guy Fawkes in boots, a dark cloak, and a wide-brimmed hat.

HOLIDAY TRADITIONS:

"GUY" (gai): likeness or dummy of Guy Fawkes

BONFIRE (BON-fi-er): large, outdoor fire

PARKIN (PAR-kin): gingerbread cake made of oatmeal and molasses or treacle

Bonfire

Parkin

MAKE A "GUY"
YOU WILL NEED:

- Sweatpants
- String
- Long-sleeve shirt
- Lots of newspaper
- Black permanent marker
- Pillowcase
- Clothespins
- A hat
- Gloves
- Boots

INSTRUCTIONS:
Tie the bottom of the pants legs with string. Tie the bottom of the shirt and the ends of the shirt sleeves with string. Stuff the pants and shirt with newspaper that is loosely balled up; then tuck the bottom of the stuffed shirt into the waist of the pants and pin the sections together. Next, fill an old pillowcase with newspaper to make a head, and tie off the opening. Draw eyes, nose, a mouth, and a mustache on your stuffed pillowcase. Push the bottom of the stuffed head into the shirt collar, and attach it with pins. Rest your guy against the wall or on a chair and add a hat, gloves, and boots. Then, on November 5th, throw a party in honor of saving England from the sneaky Guy Fawkes. Keep your "Guy" as a souvenir of the holiday.

England

LATERNENFEST (LANTERN FESTIVAL)—GERMANY

Laternenfest, the lantern festival in Germany, is celebrated on St. Martin's Day, November 11, and is a popular holiday for German children. It marks the day in the fourth century when Martin, a soldier in the Roman army, was traveling on horseback and came across a beggar in the street. The beggar did not have proper clothes for the cold weather, so Martin cut his cloak into two pieces and gave one half to the man. Later Martin was honored as a saint, a holy person who in the Christian church is worthy of special honor.

On St. Martin's Day, people often sit down to a traditional meal of roasted goose or duck, red cabbage, and dumplings. A favorite holiday treat is the traditional Weckmann, a sweet roll shaped like a man to represent St. Martin. Children prepare in advance for this holiday by making paper lanterns, which they use to light their way in a nighttime parade. After sundown, they line up behind a man on horseback who is dressed up as St. Martin in a long red cloak. The children carry their lanterns through the streets, singing traditional songs into the night.

HOLIDAY TRADITIONS:

LATERNE (la-TARE-ne): lantern

MARTINSUMZUG (MAR-tins OOM-zoog): St. Martin's parade

WECKMANN (VECK-mann): sweet roll shaped like a man with raisin eyes

SEMMELKNÖDEL (ZEM-el-knuh-del): bread dumplings

GERMAN LANTERN

YOU WILL NEED:

- Medium or large balloon
- Colorful tissue paper
- Bowl
- Sponge or paintbrush
- Glue and water mixture (50/50 mix) in a paper cup
- Single-hole paper punch
- Ribbon or string
- 1 LED tea light
- 1 stick

INSTRUCTIONS:

Blow up your balloon fully and tie it closed. Cut tissue paper into large squares or strips. Rest your balloon, knot down, in a bowl to hold it still. With a paintbrush or sponge, coat glue over the whole balloon except the area around the knot. Then cover the glue with tissue paper. When finished, attach a piece of string to the knot, and hang the balloon to dry. Once dry, pop the balloon and slowly remove it from inside the lantern. You should now have a hollow lantern with an opening. You may need to smooth out the sides. Using your single-hole punch, punch two holes on opposite sides of the rim of your lantern. Thread a ribbon or string through the holes and tie it to make a handle. Turn on your LED tea light and place it in the bottom of your lantern. Slide a stick under the handle of your lantern and go parading.

Weckmann

Laterne

Semmelknödel

CELEBRATE!

Now that you have explored a world of celebrations, you're ready to throw your own holiday party! Choose your favorite holiday from this book to celebrate, or invent your own. Would your holiday have a special ceremony? Would you dress up in costume? Would you make certain foods? What about a parade with music and dancing? If you're struggling to come up with ideas, think about what's important to you. In the end, that's what holidays are really about—taking the time to honor something meaningful. Invite your friends over to join you, and get the celebration started!

GLOSSARY

Altar: a platform or table for worship

Ancient: very old or from a long time ago

Ancestor: a family member who lived in the distant past

Anniversary: a date that is celebrated because a special event happened on that day in the past

Colony: a distant territory belonging to one nation or country

Culture: the beliefs and social practices of a group

Equality: the state of being equal, the same in importance

Fast: to not eat or drink for a period of time

Festive: cheerful, exciting

Fortune: results that occur by chance, that one has no control over

Gourd: a fruit with a hard shell and seeds that grows on a vine

Holy: respected as special or related to God

Independence: freedom from outside control

Liberty: being free and independent

Mosque: a Muslim place of worship

Muslim: a person whose religion is Islam

Plot: (verb) to plan something secretly; (noun) an evil or unlawful plan

Prophet: a person who delivers messages from God

Religious: Living according to the rules of a faith or religion

Saint: in Christianity, a holy person worthy of special honor

Synagogue: a Jewish house of worship

Tax: money people have to pay to the government

Treason: the crime of trying to destroy a government or kill a government leader

Tribe: a group of people who share the same language and customs

Worship: to honor and respect God, especially by prayer

Ofrenda with Calaveras

"Eid Mubarak!"